JONNY ZUCKER has played in several bands and worked
in radio, and as a stand-up comedian and a teacher. He started
writing full-time and has now written over thirty books for adults,
teenagers and children. These include the Venus Spring books
for Piccadilly Press and the Max Flash series for Stripes.
In addition to the Festival Time! series, he has also written
Dan and the Mudman and *Striker Boy* for Frances Lincoln.
He lives in London with his family.

JAN BARGER COHEN's previous titles include *Bible Stories
for the Very Young*, and the Little Animals series.

For Fiona and Jake – J.Z.
To Geoffrey and Audrey – J.B.C.

First published in Great Britain in 2002 by
Frances Lincoln Limited, 4 Torriano Mews,
Torriano Avenue, London NW5 2RZ

www.franceslincoln.com

First paperback edition 2003

A catalogue record for this book is available from the British Library.

ISBN: 978-0-7112-2016-4

Printed in China

5 7 9 8 6

FESTIVAL TIME!

Apples and Honey

A Rosh Hashanah Story

Jonny Zucker

Illustrated by Jan Barger Cohen

F

FRANCES LINCOLN
CHILDREN'S BOOKS

It's Rosh Hashanah –
the Jewish New Year.
I'm trying on my
brand new jumper.

Before dinner, we eat
apples dipped in honey
for sweet times ahead.
Delicious!

We crunch through the leaves
on our way to synagogue.
Our friends smile and
wave at us.

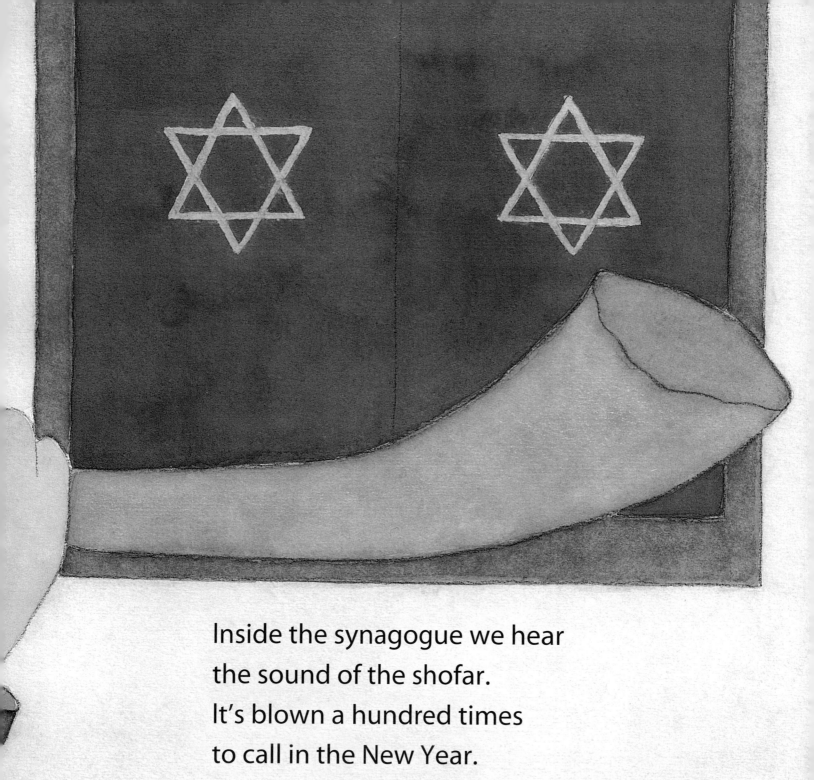

Inside the synagogue we hear
the sound of the shofar.
It's blown a hundred times
to call in the New Year.

For the ceremony of Tashlich, we say goodbye to the sad things from last year by throwing crumbs into the river.

Everyone tries a piece of pomegranate. As we munch through the seeds, we think of next year and all the kind things we want to do.

We walk outside and gaze
at the beautiful new moon.
It shines down on us,
bringing our brand new year.

What is Rosh Hashanah about?

Rosh Hashanah is the Jewish New Year and it is celebrated for two days. At this time, the Jewish pepole believe that God judges everyone according to how they have behaved during the year that has ended. It is a time to look back at the mistakes made in the last year, and new clothes are worn to symbolise a new beginning.

During the festival, people greet each other with the phrase 'L'shana tova', which means 'to a good year'. At the beginning of the evening meal, everyone eats a piece of apple dipped in honey. Apples and honey are a symbol of sweetness and of the hope that the coming year will be full of good things.

On the first afternoon, it is the custom to walk to the river, to say a special prayer and throw crumbs into the water. This ceremony is called *Tashlich* which means 'casting off', because throwing the crumbs symbolises the casting off of your sins. In this way, it is possible to make a fresh new start in the year to come.

On the second evening a pomegranate is often eaten: the seeds represent the many good deeds people hope to carry out in the coming year.

Blowing the shofar

On Rosh Hashanah, Jewish people go to the synagogue to pray and to hear the *shofar* being blown. The shofar is a ram's horn and it sounds a bit like a trumpet. It is very difficult to blow and takes lots of practice.

During the morning service the shofar is sounded 100 times. Four different phrases are played, and each time the name of the phrase is called out first:

Tekia – a single note
Shevarim – three notes
Terua – a series of short notes
Tekia Godola – a very long, single note
(the player has to take a really deep breath for this one!)

MORE TITLES IN THE FESTIVAL TIME! SERIES
BY JONNY ZUCKER

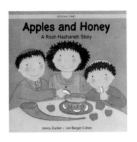

Apples and Honey – A Rosh Hashanah Story
See how a Jewish family celebrates New Year, eating apples and honey and hearing the sounds of the shofar.

It's Party Time! – A Purim Story
A story about how a family celebrates Purim: dressing up in costume, giving presents and making lots of noise!

Eight Candles to Light – A Chanukah Story
Follow a family as they light the *menorah*, open presents and eat *latkes*.

Lanterns and Firecrackers – A Chinese New Year Story
Follow a family as they let off firecrackers, watch lion and dragon dances and hang up lanterns to celebrate the start of their New Year.

Four Special Questions – A Passover Story
Read about matzah, the Seder plate, the four questions and the hunt for the Afikoman.

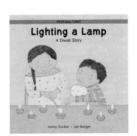

Lighting a Lamp – A Diwali Story
Follow a family as they make rangoli patterns, light divas and watch a brilliant firework display to celebrate their amazing festival of light.

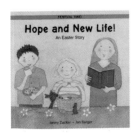

Hope and New Life! – An Easter Story
Follow a family as they take Holy Communion, eat hot cross buns, go on an Easter egg hunt and watch a big parade.

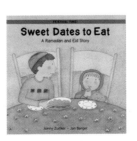

Sweet Dates to Eat – A Ramadan and Eid Story
Follow a family as they fast each day, go to the mosque on the Night of Power, and enjoy a delicious feast.

Frances Lincoln titles are available from all good bookshops.
You can also buy books and find out more about your favourite titles,
authors and illustrators on our website: www.franceslincoln.com